Contents

Words, Words, Words

V.S WoodRaven

DJS LEGACY

WORDS, WORDS, WORDS

V.S Woodraven is a young author from the east coast, currently residing in the midwest. Throughout her life Woodraven has struggled finding ways to use her voice. Growing up in theater and music Woodraven fell in love with storytelling, particularly tragedies and love stories as is now visible in her own work. The childhood books Woodraven says ignited her passion for reading and literature are *The Twilight Saga, The Bell Jar, The Shatter Me Series, Fahrenheit 451, Wuthering Height,* and *Pride and prejudice.* She admires these books for their ability to paint true pictures of strong female emotions accurately and brutally while also holding readers captive by their incredible love stories and tales of loss. This is Woodraven's first published work and she is greatly looking forward to continuing this journey with her readers.

Socials
Instagram: v.s_woodraven
Gmail: Woodravenofficial.com
For more, go to: Amisguidedthought.com

Forward

If some of these read like a hurting young girl wrote them, it's because she did. If, much later in my book, you start to see a new writer, a young woman holding the pen. It's because I didn't give up. I am unafraid of what I say because I know how it ended. The most important thing to note is the first act; it is angry and unforgiving, questioning God and self, trying to reconcile heartbreak and mistreatment, but as we move to the second act, you can see the switch. While heartbreak and pain are still notable, they are no longer the focus of my life, and I begin to experience new things like hope and joy. We begin to see self-reflection and reconciliation. So, while the first act may be hard to get through, nothing positive in life is initially made that way for most people; it takes work and pain, and we cannot be afraid of the emotions we feel during those hard times. This is proof of those experiences and validation for complex emotions. For anyone reading this, afraid of the dark things in your mind, if you are young or old and do not have the strength to say how you feel... let me do it for you. We keep going; we keep speaking because we deserve a voice. You deserve a voice. You deserve to feel comfortable in your mind. In this book, darkness and pain are present. It's not for everyone, but for everyone out there who feels like they are too dark to shine. Here is my pain, my gift to you, because you are never alone. We keep burning.

All my love,

V.S

1

Ignited

My Sunshine.

That scorching light.
I'm running and running toward something that's mine
but I am stuck in darkness.
So I stopped running.
A light I had always followed and now, I abandon it.
How long will I stand here watching it leave me be-
hind.
12.15.23

2

See Me

I hope when God stares into my soul he sees something special. Does he look and see that my greatest fear is to be nobody? Does he see I'm frightened that I am just as ordinary as I feel? Does he even care a little that I might be slipping… into Nothing?

12.18.23

3

Lethargia

I have so many things that I would rather be doing But productivity and practicality all but drop dead as soon as I am home. When my eyes flutter shut, my dreams die. When my heart stills, the chase slackens. Alas, I shall arise and serve those who waste their precious, precious time. Utterly oblivious to me, wasting away inside.

11.6.23

4

America

A flame all my life. Smothered, as I face humanity. Sticky darkness molded to my brain, carving away at its sanity. Slurped up by a groveling society. Burning, alone and empty, As the hatred of men consumes me...

12.17.23

5

Long Time, No See

No one is ever enough to make someone else change. I think you were the villain all along, and I spent years making you worse, like a soured fairy tale to my own happy ending. Maybe I was the villain because I dangled my love around you to get you to change, knowing you couldn't. I wonder if I dodged the same bullet you tried to bury in yourself. I wonder if we were two rocks sinking to the ocean floor. Holding onto each other.

1.20.24

6

Bad Turtle

Don't you ever get tired of biting the hand that feeds you? Oh, rebellious snapping turtle. Only coming up for air to attack everyone around you. One day, you'll be the only creature in that pond starving to death while the rest of the world looks away. Maybe you deserve just that.

5.22.23

7

Tested

The anger of a little Girl, bombastically terrifying and raw Could never counter the cold and calculated rage of a woman, Who has always been too much for people but never enough for the rest.

5.15.23

8

You Didn't Deserve That

Do you ever get tired of holding it in? That sorrow, that rage? The guilt? Forgiving the selfish people who lit you only to blow you out time after time. How could you not forgive that small child who just wanted to feel warm? But you forgave them, making a thousand useless excuses. Wound so tight a simple word could topple all the clean-cut walls surrounding her subconscious. Let go, girl. You may still know peace. But probably not, so why fucking bother.

12.16.23

9

You Didn't Deserve That (continued)

One day, you'll have to swallow the guilt before it climbs your throat and scratches out your eyes. Let go, they say. Forgive and pray. Ignorant of the pain, pain from those who deserve... Oh, how I wish death would soothe hate.

12.15.23

10

Stuck

Two wrongs don't make a right. But will one hundred thousand prayers begin to atone for my anger? Who will forgive first? God or the little girl who relives the same things over and over and over and over and over and...

11.6.23

11

Why

I give,and I give until I am empty. I have bumps and bruises that will not heal, I have little band-aids you peel. When do you think these scabs will turn into scars? I think my mind is just a place for you to pick when you're bored.

11.6.23

12

Wishful Thinking

Where are those who hold you like the world is crumbling and talk to you like time is running out? I want a place where sweet kisses and holding hands are enough to make you feel okay. No one will understand how badly I want to release everything in my brain to someone who will listen and not tear me apart.

6.30.21

13

What is it...

My heart has Casanova's My simple heart imploded Of all the thoughts left in my brain to you, they are now devoted. Controller of my body, the teaser of my mind. Your hands so firm, but voice so kind, Be mine, be mine, be mine. I'm dying for exposure, for I am nothing but water, Beginning to boil over.

12.15.23

14

...About love?

Y our stare holds so much tension, causing a violent snap in my attention. Oh, what is it about love, About lovers, That we dedicate our souls to the very idea of it. It's such a delicate and violent thing. Such a terrifying and tragic beast... How does one so strong, hold one so stiff with love? What is it in love that makes the tiniest action spellbinding? What is it about intimacy that feels like drinking starlight and stealing time?

12.15.23

15

Two Ships

As water fills these metal lungs and curses leave thy sailor's tongue, Oh, if that bell he would have rung, a freedom song he would have sung. But instead he stood and watched. His life, though God's, would soon be stopped. A new song now he'll adopt, "The burning of these ships must not be witnessed." Damn those ships they had to kiss and perish in eternal bliss, And captain's eyes that could not miss, the burning, Of two ships.

- July 2023

16

Fire on the playground

Imagination turned to cinders, My nightmares lit the match. If ever days did fair, a break I hope to catch. My psyche was loose, my hopes unbound, running toward the playground. Did he feel my body slinging? From the chains he used for swinging? The pieces that are left are now bent and twisted down. Caught and bound my playground now a place of ice and fire. Hollow birds crept near to ask, "What is the light we found?" The Earth did spit and fire back, "It's flame on the playground." Fingers lazy tracing round, The ashes of my mind His hands did grip and steal away, The peace I'd hoped to find.

-August 2023

17

Playground massacre

We used to play pretend. We used to pretend we were strong and scared of nothing. Now, we are stuck between stale romance and smoke. Where did the playground go? I want to swing and climb. I want my life to be mine. I want to pretend until I am dead.

-February 2023

18

Stories and Fantasies

I am a narcissist who has hyper-romanticized her whole world just to feel important. The torture of a never ceasing dream, that is only ever a dream. I love you, I love you, I love you, but it's not real and I will wake up soon. A real person I drew up and made to play sick games in my head. I'm sorry to have wasted your time. Especially when you're
not real.

-August 2023

19

I Don't Know.

I don't know what I want. I don't know what I'm feeling, but it doesn't stop. It just won't. I can't let go. But how badly I want to be happy. I shouldn't have to beg for it. I work for free, but I won't go grovel. I can't settle, and yet I feel so calm. Such little things, but I always want them, and I want someone to notice. I don't know what I want, but how tired I am of asking.

- July 2023

20

Suffocation

Suffocation is a strange feeling to adapt to. Feeling your heart strain and convulse. In a sick way, it reminds you that you're still human. Still breakable. I overanalyze everything, you, myself. What you think, how I feel, and how whatever you think always impacts how I feel. The stinging in my lungs is slowly taking over my body, and all I can do is lay on the floor and try futilely not to explode. Trying not to throw shrapnel and glass throughout my tired soul. Everything is on fire, and to put me out I've been tossed to sea with weight on my ankles, And I'm no longer suffocating, I'm drowning.

7.6.21

21

Drowning

I' m drowning in thought and the water is beginning to fill my mouth and my lungs are taunting me with the thought of a big breath, reminding me over and over again of that sweet release.

Sadly, my lungs have been taken out of communication with my body for so long that they've forgotten that I am always holding my breath.

Waiting, for life to finally let me breathe.

I keep holding and holding.

And I just keep praying someone will finally let me exhale.

Please,

please,

Let me taste the sweet air.

Please,

please,

Let me exhale.

1.17.24

22

Preface to Nothing

I loath a life where I pour my life into pages upon pages of
sorrow with no reader.

Kindness is weakness and souls are built just to be
crushed.

There is no more peace.

I dance in the whirlwind of chaos.

Where is the place for the brokenhearted?

Where do the Red Eyes go to weep?

6.20.21

23

Nothing

I hate this.
I hate cruel women,
I hate spineless men,
I hate little girls with no confidence,
I hate that I am one of those girls.
Hate breaks my heart,
So I break over and over again, unrecognizable after each reconstruction.
I hate that I will never outrun my hurt.
I hate the mere 26 letters I have to express myself, it is not enough.
I gobble nouns and sounds and vomit up my stupid feel-ings.
I hate that no one will ever read them and understand.
Most of all I hate that no one has ever tried.
6.24.21

24

Fresh

Can we start over?
Can we try again once we've gone and failed?
Is there any redemption for love?
For something so deep and wrong?
I blurred the lines and all I can see now is your disap-
pointed face staring at me.
I dream about what it could have been.
God how bad I wanted it, how clearly I saw it,
How fresh it smells and how horrible it is,

25

Forbidden Waters

I am new blood in old waters
A stale drop in a stagnant pond.
There is whiskey in my system I did not drink and yet I
am so intoxicated.
You are age and wisdom,
You are the radiance of darkness,
You smell like a fresh sea that I want to drown in.
I do not fear the water halting air when I look at you.
I do not fear my head going under.
I am, however, petrified of the sharks in this bay cir-
cling me.
Doubt like sharp teeth scraping my mind and eating
restful sleep.
This blood would spill for you,
My soul set aflame for you,
My lungs scream for you, though I make no sound.
My skin trembles violently at the thought of you.
What a beautiful ocean, what a deadly sea.

I am in love with you, though parts of me say I shouldn't
be.

11.6.23

Page Break

Interactive Questionare

What's something you've never told anyone?

How are you feeling?

Are you where you want to be? Do you feel like you're being held back?

Have you ever given up on a dream, if so, what?

What do you want to do with your life?

26

I still wonder

Is it love if all you want to do is hold their hand? Is it obsession that stirs the need to simply look into their eyes to feel satisfaction? Isn't it crazy to sit by him like a dog waiting to be petted? Complacently sitting. While you get nothing? Disappointment is my new lover but I wonder, what would it be like to be yours?

11.20.23

27

Fly in a web

I like the ache, I love thrumming numbness, I adore the stillness it brings to my heart, my body. No matter the cracking. Darkness hugs better than any man. Sorrow kisses better than any lover. Why would I arise from a web where I don't have to feel anything... Why should I fear the bite, Of the spider I created? I am not afraid, of venom from my own teeth.

12.3.23

28

The Comfort Of A Safe Place

Why is everything different here in the dark? When the sun goes away and eyelids fall shut. It's here in this place I come alive. It is something so... sensual. Something enters my soul, something raw and hot, something so very, very alive. Maybe it's all my thoughts coming out to play with each other to feel and bite one another. Fear, leaving my body My eyelids heavy, and my lips parted for no one. The very rhythm of my body in a trance that terrifies me and I cannot help but surrender. I think perhaps in this place, this place I don't have to hide how very much I want to live...

8.1.21

29

Hope

I caught it. I've locked it in my chest and it's burning its way through me. Violating my soul and shaking my very core. "Do you feel this?" it whispers, "Can you feel this the way I do?" How funny this feeling chooses right now, in this moment to make me explode. The euphoria and the strength of it , the sheer depth. I think, maybe, this has been waiting for me since the beginning of all my suffering.

8.21

30

A different type of Heartbreak

I watch his eyes and I sense I'm completely visible to him. No part of me is foggy or mysterious. No matter how I change. I know his heart is mine, I will always be his. Sometimes though I wonder, is there a point I will change so much he doesn't recognize me… When I'm not the girl he married but the woman he sees, will he still love me? Will love be different? Stronger, hotter, tangible. Will sense turn on me, cold? Or will I be forced to wander the perimeters of my own damn shadow? Could I stretch the folds of gray to mold around my new form? I am new and teeming, craving this new world, tasting and devouring very strange things. Even if this world is not mine, I will conquer it. My only fear is that I will conquer alone.

11.17.23

31

Something or rather.

I don't always feel the way I want to. I sometimes don't get the luxury of blowing off what I feel quickly enough for it to not make an impact. Try as I may to not regard my feelings, they are always there, lurking. Feelings, in that way, are non-consensual. They push and paw until they are at the epicenter of my brain and on the tip of my tongue. I rarely feel like I have a choice. I barely have the self-control to fight them. It would make things so much easier, I think, if my emotions were not always written on my face. I do not know why I feel the things I do but I would really like to.

12.17.23

32

Number Thirty-Seven

D ark romance is brutal. Roses, daggers, candles. All black and stars. Solitary longing and whispers. At its very core is longing for something that may very well kill you. There is danger and heartbreak but you're willing to die for it. The brutality of it is fascinating. The idea that you may never get what you want, that you burn a lonely flame forever. More than admiring from afar it's... starving from afar. So many of us just want the love but it is us sickos that yearn for the bleeding romance tucked inside the books we hide.

11.17.23

33

19

I am so old but so young. So seemingly inexperienced but inside a library of stories, closed and unfinished chapters. I do not see it as a point of pride, yet youth is seen as a point of weakness. I am as strong as any other and just as broken. I don't remember being young, only so naive. My body feels the weight of the things I carry, the bags under my eyes so heavy. If I was forced to grow up to not be hurt by the ignorance of people older and younger than me, where do I fit in?

1.17.24

34

Storm Dancer

There is rain and there are storms. To each my soul answers. Where mist and cold swirl, You'll find my heart entangled in its waltz. Tethered to a cloud and teased by droplets. A smile tugs at me from deep inside. The only time sadness creeps in, Is when the sun eats my dance partner and evaporates the orchestra. Cold and foggy, I dream. Wet and floating I sing.

12.22.23

35

Speechless

I say nothing; your silence echoes. Skull-shattering silence rings deep in me. Speaking to you is such an exhausting event you don't bother to do it at all. Conversations run together, but you've been shot in the knees. Am I not an adversary for your words? Simply a lackluster sparring partner? I swore to stop giving myself to people who don't want me. It's entirely my fault for making a friend out of drywall.

12.29.23

36

Sea Spray

Big gulps of salt water, The view of the sea, So many dark things it settles in me. Laughter bellowing, a sound I must save. The crashing of waves. To these sounds, my heart craves. I want not the ponds, not the small murky puddles, I need the whole damn ocean to turn me into rub-

ble.

1.24.24

37

Tread Lightly

I cannot swim in still water, not without thrashing waves or a tempting current. The stillness unnerves me. Treading and paddling an act of survival, Icey water taking my breath away. I need chaos to keep me afloat. Treading and floating because I cannot give up. Kicking and bobbing because I know no other way to swim.

1.16.24

38

Oh, my friend.

I imagine no smile. No laughter when he took you. Took from you. I can only imagine that strangers' face. Only ache in cold understanding and hot anger. I think of that voice that might have yelled. I don't know the whole story. It's not mine to tell, but people who hurt people deserve nothing but hell. Crazy to think, we hate ourselves more than the men and women who lay their disgusting hands on us. I don't know if you fought back, But I did not. We are not weak, Because we are still here, And we are still try-ing.

1.21.24

39

Good times

There are gaps in time and I am slipping through them. Holes in the universe and I dip into them. Nothing feels better than total oblivion.

1.1.24

40

3 a.m

Surely, Surely you must know. I am achingly in love with you. You absolutely have to know, I hate breathing without you. If you know, Then you certainly must know how I fear exhaling when you're not here. Only for fear of losing a single breath of you. Obviously I tremble. Quietly I yearn.

1.20.24

41

It's Good To See You (A Poem For A Poem)

Quiet, crazy thing. You may not have liked who you were in the school where we met, But just like now, We are intertwined weeds in a bed of prideful posies You bring the light into the world that illuminates my dark world. You are the bursts of color, I am the wilting of leaves. What a friendship. What a coincidence we find each other again, after all those years.

11.22.24

42

Porcelain

Vomiting, Seeing what a disgusting person I am on the inside. Viewing the vile and dinner that couldn't stand digesting in the pits of me. Meat that couldn't stand to grace me with nutrients. I would throw myself up and out of me if I could. An aftertaste, tangy and wool like on my teeth. Hot breath, fresh hate slipping from my lips.

1.23.24

43

WAKE UP

The ringing hits me first, Then everything dances around me. A horrifying ballet. My world fades, eaten by a bright, bright light. All I see is burning white. My eyes are shut but under my lids is a monster. It wants me, wants to eat my very being. It's hot claws squeeze my brain, a vibrating numb sensation. Bells, bells with their ceaseless ringing. And suddenly, Everything is black and I am shaking. So terrified I am dead. So certain that I am drifting in a pool of black, barely floating. Hands, all over me pulling me out, soaked in my fear. Heaving out the darkness that made its way down my throat. I'm starving, Like that horrible light ate up all my sated pleasure. It keeps coming back, eating at more and more of me. Taking its time with me, stretching time to torture me, devouring me into the light. It feels like death, and she does not take you peacefully. I've felt it so many times but never mastered my fear. I am not the conquer of death, but its mistress, a sad, sullied servant.

And I am so scared, so unbelievably scared it will always
hunt me. Only next time, I won't wake up.

1.24.24

44

The Leap

My hands grow cold at the thought of it... I wasn't fair to you, and I know it. A sick, desiccated thing my mind is. A blind, misguiding thing my heart has grown to be. I can't guess the life I would have had. Though now I try to paint it. I see something beautiful. But, I know. I know it would not have ended well. Because of me. It has hurt people terribly, The way I've painted them. I have always made my colors too bright, too angular, and impossible. Then I burn them. While the oils are still wet and my heart is not broke. Mostly because I once refused to see the beauty in darkness and was frightened of silence. Now the only sound in my mind is the swish of a brush while a distant heart is breaking.

1.31.24

45

The Jump

There are things I cannot let go of. Faults that are mine, cracks that do not fill. As a part of me as my soul. There's no distraction for proper pain. You bathe in it or suffocate within it. I cannot find anything to fill the cracks where you chipped off. Or fell out, Because I could not take care of you.

1.31.24

46

The Fall

You should have just told me, while I was singing and dreaming. Too blinded by sound to see danger. That I was killing you. I am not cruel, though deep down, I knew. I hated you because I could not understand. Now I see, While your soul cried out, I sang along and thought nothing of it.

1.31.24

47

To Be Human

We Fight our whole lives for identity only to be disappointed by who we choose to be. We sink in love we think we deserve. Weighted by dreams we share with no one. We consume ourselves, searching for the beauty right in front of us. We die in our minds before we find peace in our bodies.

5.23.24

48

I Wonder

I wonder if I stared at you long enough I'll find what it is that makes me search for you in every crowd. I wonder when you don't look at me, If you know how hard my heart slams against my ribs in an attempt to reach you. Sometimes, it feels like you're content to let it beat me to death.

3/1/24

49

I Don't Care You Didn't Stay

I wish I could look you in the face and mine would not give me away. I want you to see cold indifference, The face of someone not utterly impacted by you. If our eyes met, I'd want a breeze of recognition. Not the sting of pelting ammunition. You don't get to see the smile I made for you, Because you didn't see the tears I split for you. I want you to see my face and not see that i thought my child's eyes, Would be green.

3/6/24

50

Exhaustion

I run myself ragged thinking about you. My eyes are sick of looking at you. My soul is losing its tenacity. But still, for some, Masochistic, stupid reason. I am still running to someone who always walks away.

3.1.24

51

Hello

I've had all the brightness sucked out of me, Now that I'm twenty. The gray, the steam clouds all that now cover me. There's nothing to be, No one to play, I just get tired of feeling this way.

2.5.24

52

Heal

I can keep some parts of me to myself. Because I deserve that, I deserve a part of me that is just mine. I will dig through the depths of myself to find them. I will face the ugly and love it. I will lay with my pain and let it heal. I will be whole again. Whole. Then maybe my art won't be so lonely.

3.17.24

53

New and Hungry

I think maybe I'll be hungry forever. Starving for the very something that makes us humans feel full. I'm scared, though, that if I found it, I would still not be satisfied.

4.1.24

54

One Day

One day someone will see the age in my eyes. Recognize that I am no child. As I've watched the world wilt and grow. Felt the very real weight of twenty years on a person. I have watched stars hang dead in our galaxy. I've felt the stagnation of people thrice my age and wondered how it is that a person doesn't grow, but will mock the growing left in others. For I have never seen a child and laughed at what the world will do to it. I have only looked and hoped they won't be as insulted as I have been. Maybe instead of sneering, we should smile and hold onto each other so we do not feel so terribly young and terribly lonely at the same time.

4.16.24

55

Why Not?

Can we not just love unconditionally, without expectation?! Can I not just kiss you for all my worth, so you will see how much I care for you? Can we not watch the stars together, once? Then decide for ourselves if we are a disaster. Because I would keep loving you, Even if that love did not make it to sunrise.

4.13.24

56

Names

Because of all this, I can say I finally feel myself. I know her. A new friend though she was never quite a stranger. I will love her infinitely and guard her eternally.

3.26.24

57

Eternal Emptiness

To hold a little bit of everyone you love, Is to leave a little bit of yourself with them. Eventually, if you're not careful, you have nothing left, But the love of everyone else but yourself.

4.20.24

58

Yesterday

One day, maybe when I'm thirty or forty, I'll look back and think I was so silly. Even now though, I see that ten year old. I see the world she's grown into, But yet I cannot fault her for thinking she is so old. When everyone always praised her, for being such a mature little girl. Who was always so well-behaved.

4.16.24

59

The Multi-thread

I have painted you into a pretty picture no one could possibly live in, A pretty piece of the world where you are perfect from every angle. It's like playing God the way we make people up in our heads to be someone they just aren't. The innocent intention may be there, But we are simply humans, a mess of emotions and thoughts. We cannot be sculpted or scribbled.

4.7.24

60

Human Heart

I cannot change this, It's not healthy to obsess. I need to focus on myself. Stop Daydreaming. Stop dreaming in general. You had to smile at me like that. Twice, unknowingly. I could paint it. I loved it so much. That makes me a horrible person.

4.7.24

61

The Sword

I am of the sword. Living and dying by my own strength, my own words. Double-sided and sharp. My mind is hot, freshly forged, being molded into something magnificent. My thoughts are like steel, heavy but beautiful, deadly but shining.

4.21.24

62

Lightning Flashed

The thought hit me so hard. The realization it doesn't sit in your heart like it does mine. That it does not burn in your veins. Walking, running, away from you took so long. Hurt so bad. I suppose I should be grateful it caused you nothing, you felt, nothing. That you did not, do not see the valleys between us. It was love, obviously. Plane as day. Bright as sunshine. There was no bushel, not a switch to turn it off. It could not even be dimmed. Nor snuffed, not by anyone. It was relentless, if not wicked. Sorrow's pursuit chased me out of bed. You're sleeping well. While I ran like hell. I don't know how long the journey would take. I just need to get there, soon. A gunshot. And this mind started racing. My fingers trying to keep pace. I ran for my life. Wrote for my soul.

5.19.24

63

Green

I like to look at things like I'm seeing them for the last time. Taking in details like I'll die tomorrow. Smelling the air adds scent to the memory. So one day, when I don't remember, the smell may bring me back And the picture won't be so fuzzy.

5.5.24

64

Bonfire

A sad song with drums and tears. Out here in the wilderness, I know not what to fear. Men and bears are the same to me. Either way these hippies and I we, we are free. There are stories here, real and fake. Different names, a brand new place. When I go home I'll remember who's lucky. Not the rich men in their homes But the hippies, and the places they go.

5.7.24

65

Those Hippies

When the hippies said, "You don't need to carry that here." I know they meant my gear, but on the inside, I felt it. I felt the release of everything I was holding. Too tired to try to be everything I expect of myself. I walked around in my bra. I ate ramen and doughnuts and drank excessive amounts of coffee. I said Hello to everyone and laughed at everything. There was no reason to hide. So I stayed for days in the weightlessness of nature.

5.8.24

66

Blow

There was a tornado in the area, Maybe you saw it? About two-hundred miles an hour, ripping up all your flowers. It originated in my house, where clouds were circling, and I was thinking. Thinking, no one would miss me if I simply took off with the wind. So if you saw that tornado in the area, rushing about two-hundred miles an hour, Don't panic, for it was only me, trying to fly away. Sadly, I just ripped up all your pretty flowers. Oh, how my advancement towards freedom does vex you.

5.24.24

67

Cracked

The incompleteness of me is so sore. Stretching out the kinks in me aches tremendously. I hold the insides of myself tightly because yes, there is pain. But it is mine. I may no longer smile wholly, or laugh as soundly to strangers, though why should I? Why are we expected to bare our souls to people who do not deserve it? I say the world doesn't need to know the life I lead, that sorrow is as intoxicating as joy to me. Historians do not need to comprehend that I feel everything. They simply need to know I survived you, and the ache is wholly mine now. That I exist in this world and it is still as beautiful as can be imagined through cracked lenses.

6.2.24

68

We're All Aflame

I am not for everyone. I am not easily digested. I offer my hurt to you as a gift. I write heartburn for your soul. Because it is the only beauty I offer, For those who were never afraid of fire.

6.2.24

69

Self

Individuality can make a person so lonely. Men searching for independence. Woman yearning for acceptance. Count me with the many who forget, I'm not the only one in the world trying to be somebody.

6.2.24

70

Proximity

You should know, Love existed for you in me. A hole carved by you, nurtured by proximity. I mean, of course it was because now you're gone and that hole throbs. It is tortured and angry. Even when it was over, your lips uttered not a word. So I loved another and am sorry for the both of us.

7.4.24

71

The Curse

I write because it must be said. Penning because the words want to be read. Time is my enemy, taunting me till it's fed. I type endlessly, I shout to those who will hear All my words I hold dear.

7.1.24

72

Riddle Of Water

Y ou've heard it. Your head has popped up at the call, your heart has stilled with its trickle. People have died to it, some are born in it. Life and death revolves around the one gift we get for free but so freely take for granted. I wonder, how can you pollute the thing that soothes you? How can you defile the water you danced in as a child?

7.2.24

73

Fear and Happiness

I have this fear of happiness. I've felt how bright it burns in you but how cold it leaves you. The quicker its departure the heavier the dread that it won't come back. If love was like happiness, if it fled that fast I wouldn't wonder why no one loves at all. I have felt love without happiness, I've felt love starve and yearn but loved it all the same. The lack of happiness is so much less endearing, there is only a gnawing sense you've done something terribly wrong. Damn the temptress who flaunts her easy joy. Cruise the mistress who elopes with it.

6.28.24

74

Hearsay

They say it comes and goes in waves, Loss, pain, anger. But these have been the most constant of companions for me. There will always be a ripple in my pond, a storm in my sea. I am the captain of this ship, master of chaos and this, too, I will weather.

6.24.24

75

The Ugly Truth

I wish more people could talk honestly and take the honesty given to them. Brutal, frustrating honesty. Because honestly, I wouldn't have to write so much damned poetry.

6.10.24

76

Butcher

I am quite the slasher. A perfect rehashes. I like to rip into myself over and over. Dip my toes into the sorrow of every inconsequential moment of my life. Twenty years, oh the time. I'll look into these emotions, because they're the strongest part of me. I will peer into the hurt, until it's numb and dead and beautiful.

77

Runaway

The mountains and valleys of my mind are my favorite
place to get lost.
6.2.24

78

Girl

S have off that girl like a charm. Punch off that baby fat. Pale your freckles and grow out that hair. Anything to be a thing they stare at, rather than a woman they respect. Is this the way we'll raise our daughters? Hate who you are, envy who you're not, but never be united. I will not stand for this.

6.1.24

79

Words

I live and die by the English language. Each word is a feast. Every conversation is sustenance for my hungry soul. They are feeding me and leaving me with letters to chew on. Sometimes, the words are so sweet I think of them for dessert. Other times, the words turn sour and sit in the pit of my stomach, slowly and painfully making me wish I had never heard a syllable.

5.2.24

80

Kindling

Parts of me always burn a little. Whether I'm in a mood of spiteful joy or a fit of rage, there's a fire within me I cannot contain. I decide not when it erupts nor what it engulfs.

7.27.24

81

Toxic Love

There are people in your lives whom you love wholly, They are kind and generous but sometimes wickedly self-serving. When I hear, "We accept the love we think we deserve." I think back to every little heartbreak and wonder why I felt so strongly I deserved that... I am not a toy, I am human. I have a heart and feelings and demand to be understood; if not comprehended, then respected. I want nothing less. However, I still crave the people who will only leave me empty. Eventually, I will learn to let that bit of me starve.

5.29.24

82

The Poet

I can feel my legacy as one feels ghosts… I feel it in the walls around me, breathing down my neck. "Write, write, write!" "Think, think, think!" Leave something behind. Leave anything behind. The cold hand of death is tapping my shoulder, reminding me I am running out of time. In an icy sweat, I write for those who are not born but will one day face the darkness. I will light a way so they will not be lost, the way I found Slyvia so that someone may find me. And I know, bones or not, I'll feel the tingle of someone running their hands down the cover of my book, the anticipation of another human reading the first page, and know I will never truly be lost but just waiting for someone to stumble upon me. Even now, I feel it. My future, it will burn.

4.29.24

83

Father?

It's not being stolen if you had the chance to fight for me. It's not abandonment because you were never there. I may not be the son you kept, but I am ever more a man than you.

7/16/24

84

Monster

The monster sits and pouts. Of this, I have no doubt. He'll never know what love is about. Throughout my life, I thought of you, But your shot with me, you damn well blew. All that caring I tried to do and how quickly now I feel nothing for you.

7/16/24

85

Hush Now

I gnorance, ignorance all around. Ignorance, I tell you, is
all I have found. I know it's ignorance from the sound,
Of that old man's voice going round and round.
7/27/24

86

A Cheer For Quiet

I sincerely love everyone who has taught me to be comfortable in silence. That quiet does not mean I'm upset. Being reserved doesn't make me unfriendly. I don't have to be up in my head to enjoy something other than my own voice.

7.25.24

87

My Girl and The World

Reading back my old work is like stroking the hair on the head of a hysterically sad little girl. I wrap my arms around her, letting her cry while I wipe the tears from her cold cheek. I was holding myself together because what she went through didn't break us. But she deserved someone to hold her the way I do now. I read between the lines, see her story, and kiss her forehead. I lay her down and read her stories from our future. She now rests, and I will carry us the rest of the way. In a way, sharing these poems, stories, and the little bits of my soul is like letting her be known and thus knowing we are never alone.

7.10.24

88

On The Dock

There is a distance between us that makes you the epicenter of my fossilization. Small waves lapping, beckoning, pulling back only to crash in waves of you. To cross the miles would be to leave a trail fire by the docks. I can feel the blisters on my feet and smell my hair burning. So I need to know, before it's too late, before my thoughts are ash if I were to cross the lake, would you be there with a cleat or gasoline?

7.30.24

89

The Finale

You've sifted through my thoughts and broken rambles, You have been witness to my soul and my broken heart, the utter incompleteness of me. You've bought the most vulnerable and valuable parts of me; I hope it was worth it. I hope it was nothing like you expected, but it was exactly what you needed. I hope you now know, we start with the worst of us, to get to the best of us. Reading all this, you're now a dear friend I may not even know. Goodbye for now, but not forever. You've been the seer to the most joyous of my artistic endeavors.

All my love,

V.S Woodraven

Dedication

As the pages of my first book come to a close I could not be filled with a more mixed bag of emotions. This is one of those things you always think about doing, but never complete. Something that gathers dust off a shelf and you learn to hate, but here it is. Printed, published, out into the world. Although, I have to say, while all these wound up stories come from me and my experiences there are a few people I have to thank for this book being in your hands.

Firstly, I would like to thank my family. We've been through so much that has cultivated many poems with me and I wouldn't be where I am today had I not grown up with such strong/stubborn people. Mom, you may not have always loved the sad things I have to say, but I am grateful for your support. Dad, artist to artist you have always inspired me to write what I want without fear of criticism. I love you. My husband. Thank you for not resenting the hours I spend at my desk instead of with you and thank you for never trying to hold me back from expressing something so vulnerable. My friends. Thank you Ryne and Bennett, who were some of the first people to ever read my work and give feedback. Ryne, you are gifted in all you do and I don't know what would come of me if I didn't have your kindness. Bennett, poetry isn't your thing but you never said no when I asked if you could read my newest poem, having an outsider's point of view was crucial in finding the mood I wanted this book to have. Kat and

Brannen, thank you for providing your home as an always needed relief from working and thank you for never commenting when I am nose deep in my phone writing down ideas for new poems; you have no idea how many I've written while Trunks sits on my lap begging for a Cheeto. Suddenly Hollow, though I lost a lot in losing you, this is what came from it, and I am grateful. I would like to thank my amazing publishing company, DJ Legacy Publishing Company, for taking a chance on my work and helping spread this wildfire. Last, but not least, my readers. I don't know how large of a group you are, but I want to say, from the bottom of my heart, I am so grateful to you for taking the time and energy into reading these poems. They are so much more to me than words; they're my story, wrapped in pretty words and I hope if you take away anything from these pages, we may start out angry and hopeless but we keep burning. We are the light and we are not alone.

Thank you.

All my love,

V.S Woodraven

A Look Behind
Words, Words, Words

A Look Behind
Words, Words, Words

A Look Behind
Words, Words, Words

A Look Behind
Words, Words, Words

www.ingramcontent.com/pod-product-compliance
Lightning Source LLC
Chambersburg PA
CBHW071741150726
47998CB00005B/1748